THE
TEACH YOUR CHICKEN
TO FLY

TRAINING MANUAL

THE
TEACH YOUR CHICKEN
TO FLY

TRAINING MANUAL

TREVOR WEEKES

TEN SPEED PRESS
BERKELEY, CALIFORNIA

First published in The United States 1995 by
TEN SPEED PRESS
P.O. Box 7123
Berkeley, California 94707

Copyright © Trevor Weekes 1995

All rights reserved. No part of this publication may be reproduced, stored in a
retrieval system, or transmitted in any form
or by any means, electronic, mechanical,
photocopying or otherwise, without prior
permission of the publisher.

Library of Congress
Cataloguing - in - Publication data
on file with Publisher

Designed and produced by
The Watermark Press
Sydney, Australia

Printed and bound in China

2 3 4 5 – 99 98 97 96 95

Contents

An Introduction

It is late fall and the chill of winter is drawing near. High above in the pale sunlight numerous birds are swooping, flapping their wings and practicing formation flying in preparation for their long winter migration.

What a magnificent sight they make. Will these exotic creatures return again next summer to grace the skies with their presence we wonder. And who would have believed that these birds of the sky were once birds of the ground – the fowl yard in fact! For these soaring, swooping aviary aviators about to migrate over thousands of kilometers are none other than the common fowl, known to us all as egg layers and a good all round meal.

The year 1940 was a turning point in fowl life. For this was the year in which an inventor, sympathetic to the plight of fowls who had so much to give and so much to fly for, put forward a theory to The Society for Rights for Inferior Birds. His proposition was simple. If the common chicken could be trained early, it would gradually develop wing muscles sufficient to enable it to fly at high altitudes like other birds.

Accordingly, an exercise machine was produced for use by suitable fowls and included with it were cutouts of the major

city landmarks and some of the surrounding countryside.

Considerable thought went into the development of this machine to ensure that the fowl users received both physical and mental stimulation. A Construction, Instruction, and Training Manual was issued with each machine, and for those fowls who had completed basic flight training, an extension kit could be obtained for a modest price.

Presented in this book are selections of drawings, both anatomical and aerodynamic, together with construction details of the training machine and the flight theory relevant to launching this hitherto earthbound bird.

The Beginning
(Potential Flyers)

1

As with any pursuit of excellence, it is important to take great care when selecting a fowl for flight.

If you have decided to train your own bird, please refer to Chart No. 17 (not included here) to check the measurements and vital statistics of the potential flyer. Good health is crucial to fowl flight and good eyesight is mandatory for all aviators. Have them both checked out at your local GP or veterinarian. It is also a good idea for fowl owners to have a medical check-up before embarking on the training schedule as the physical exertions required for a prolonged program can be considerable. Remember, this is not some cheap endeavor but a serious and worthwhile development of aviary science.

Only when you are completely satisfied that your chicken is ready for training should it be introduced to the equipment and be measured for a harness. For do-it-yourself enthusiasts a pattern may be obtained by writing to Department 41, Fowlair Industries, P.O. Box 7123, Berkeley, California 94707, enclosing a stamped, self-addressed envelope.

Note: Harnesses must be changed as the chickens grow. Savings on equipment may be made by buying secondhand harnesses which are often advertised in the classifieds.

Figure 1.

Quantum leaps have recently been achieved in fowl flight training programs by pre-conditioning chickens while they are still in the egg. I do not propose to enter into the age old discussion of which came first, except to note that an egg has one of the best aerodynamic shapes possible.

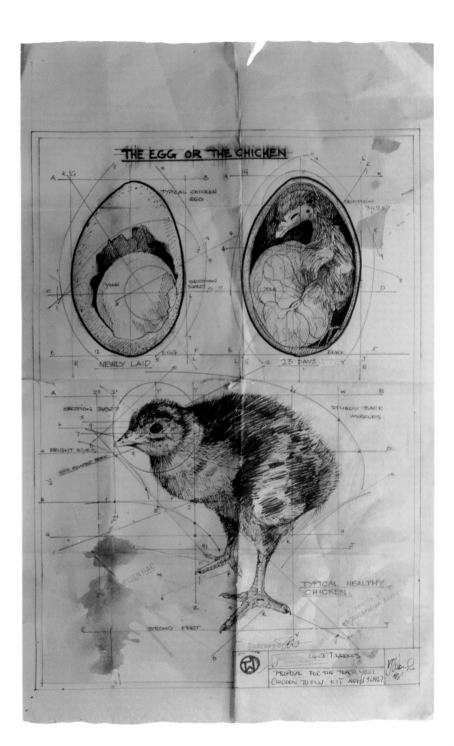

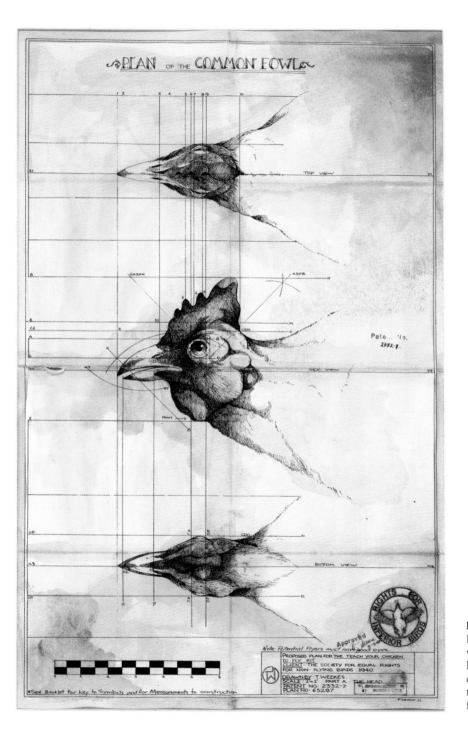

Figure 2.
Plan of head of common fowl viewed from above, below and laterally. It is interesting to make a comparison of the bird's comb with the dorsal fins of shark's and other fast moving underwater predators.

Figure 3.
By simulating the terrain over which
the chickens may expect to fly, fowl
owners can soothe the nerves of the
cadet aviators.

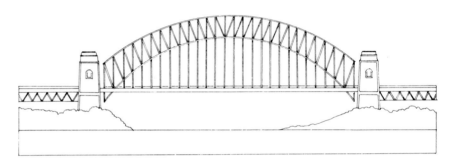

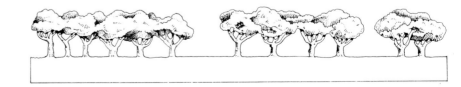

The Machine and its Parts

2

Developed from the designer's initial rough sketches, the machine has been refined to the height of perfection. Moreover it has undergone a program of rigorous testing to ensure that your chicken is provided with the best that money can buy. The mainframe is constructed of white beech wood and is guaranteed to last a lifetime. The tension-tested stainless steel wire resists corrosion in damper climates, and the harness has been softened and waterproofed with an impregnation of oil and tallow. Each machine has been handcrafted by the well-known coach building firm of Peabody and Strutt and is generally recognized to be the best that money can buy. (See specifications on page 26.)

Operation
Simultaneous rotation of the handles will transport the bird (suspended on the thin wire pulley system) backward and forward along the track.

Handles
The handles are available in white beech or can be specially made from aluminium if desired. The handles are left and right.

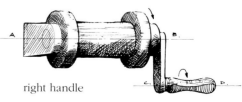

right handle

13

Pulleys

There are six pulleys. All of them are made of solid brass and the pulley holders of white beech.

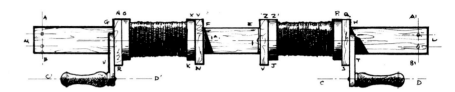

Handle Housing

Also made of white beech, the housing is designed to hold both handles and to give support to the structure.

Bracing

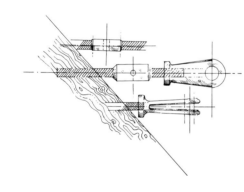

The use of turnbuckles increases strength and adds support to the outer structure. Turnbuckles are constructed in aluminum and the wire is stainless steel.

Cutouts

These are made of three-ply and the images are painted in acrylic. They are designed to enable the bird to familiarize itself with the landmarks and relate to them when it is flying at great heights. They are scaled accordingly (see Figs. 3 and 11b.)

Target

This provides something for the bird to aim for as it flies along the track of the Flying Machine. The target is of primed cotton duck and painted with acrylic.

Harness

This is made of the finest leather and is hand-tailored and personally fitted to each bird when it is ready to fly. (See Fig. 5 for plan and details of attaching harness to bird).

Harness Holder

This holder is made of white beech and houses two brass pulleys. When attached to the stainless steel track it travels along and supports the bird (see Fig. 8.)

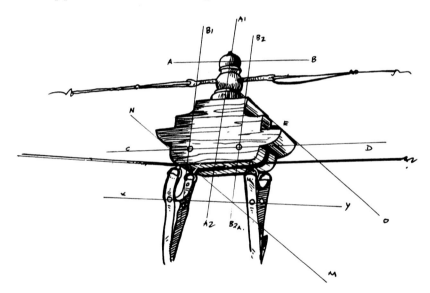

Figure 4.

The skull structure and skeletal system of the chicken. When shown in this dramatic fashion the relationship of today's common fowl with its prehistoric forebear, the pterodactyl, becomes immediately apparent.

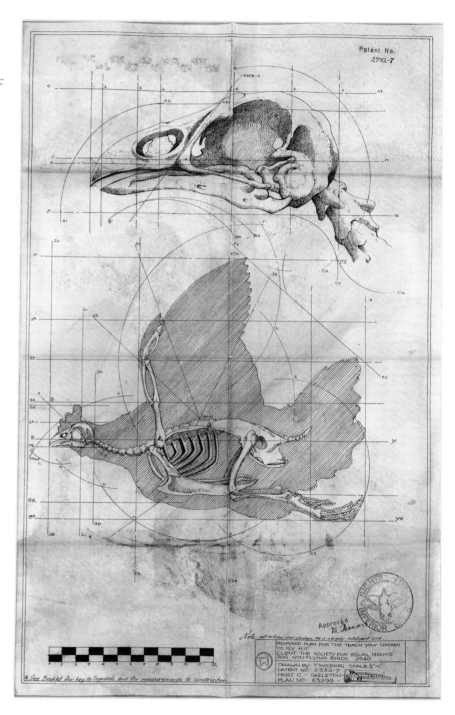

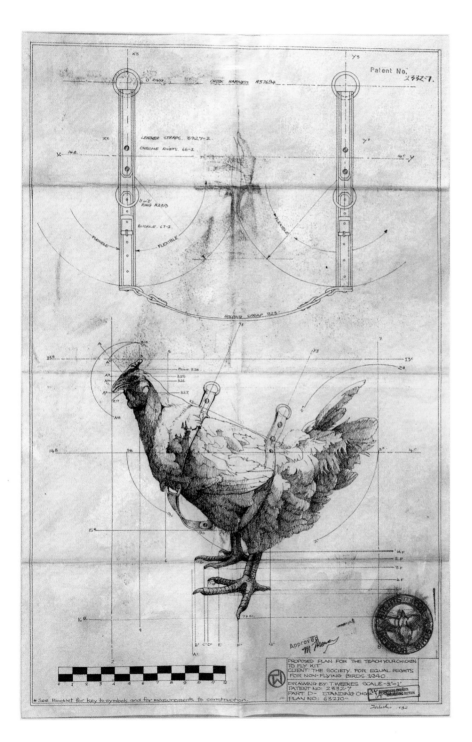

Figure 5.
Note the proud standing position of the potential flyer. The well constructed harness with its safety underbrace snuggles into the short downy underfeathers of this brave bird.

17

Figure 6.
Freud with friend! This painting by one of the major portrait painters of the day is in a private collection in Vienna. Widely recognized as a fowl lover, it was Sigmund Freud's interest in these birds which gave rise to the now widely used term "Freudian Chic."

Psychology

3

Your young chicken flyer will quite naturally feel insecure and unsure of itself. For this reason it is essential that reassurance and confidence are implanted firmly in its brain right from the beginning. Several mental exercises have been devised to instill confidence and they have all proved very successful. They are included with Kits Nos. 3 and 4.

Audio Visual Presentation

This consists of slides of bulky birds in flight (such as eagles, condors and pelicans) with which the chicken can make a mental association for size and body weight. The soundtrack includes bird noises and selected sounds of flapping wings.

Further use for A/V material

By dubbing the soundtrack from the A/V presentation and making it into a twelve minute endless tape, the chicken owner can convey the message subliminally to the trainee bird. This is best done by playing the sound of flight from small speakers hidden in the roost. The tape can be played throughout the night, thereby implanting a feeling of security in the bird's brain. Many fowl lovers have testified just how well this system works.

Although different in wingspan and beak length, the pelican which uses its wings in the most economic manner, provides an excellent role model for the aspiring chicken.

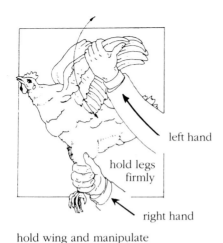

left hand

hold legs firmly

right hand

hold wing and manipulate

Muscle stimulation chart

Many owners have had great success in stimulating muscle growth in their chickens by means of wing massage. This can be affected quite simply with the aid of an assistant who holds the bird's legs. At the same time the owner can manipulate the wings in a flying motion, see diagram.

Note: This exercise should be maintained for approximately 30 minutes.

wing muscles - points of massage

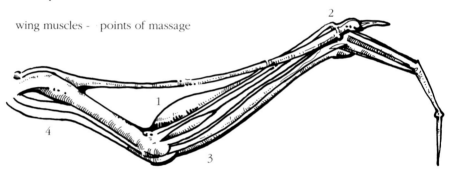

Some owners have achieved remarkable results using back projection techniques. However this is not included in the kit. Possible sources of film footage are the Army and Air Force. Projection of aerial views of places known to a chicken, while at the same time slowly rotating the Starting Machine, has proved to be a great confidence booster.

Further Reading

For the true enthusiast and concernecd chicken owner the book Manipulative Massage for the Serious Chicken Owner T. Weekes 1961, is highly recommendecl. This book is free with Kit No. 14.

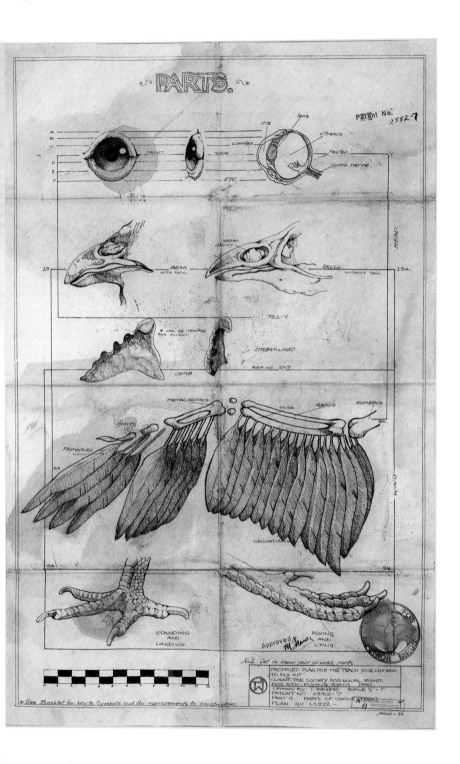

Figure 7.
Knowing a bird's parts is very important for all fowl owners. You are recommended to check them daily.

21

Figure 8.
When suspended in the harness of the Training Machine, the potential flyer presents his or her most aerodynamic aspect, ensuring correct wing and body posture in real flight. Correct alignment of the harness buckles is essential.

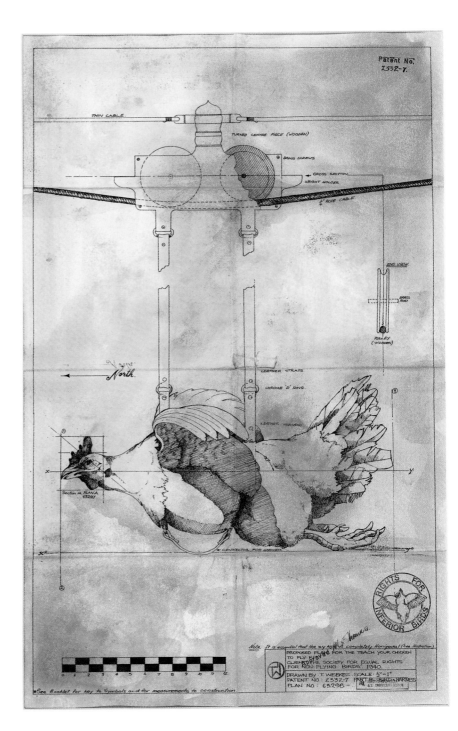

The Training and Exercise Program

4

When the machine is assembled, strap the well-briefed and enthusiastic cadet chicken flyer into the harness. A few soothing words always help allay any pre-flight fears.

Step 1. Once the chicken is settled place your feet in the position to start winding.

Step 2. Take the handles (left and right) firmly in your hands and turn them clockwise with a steady motion. Try to avoid jerking as this may upset novice flyers. Machine operators are advised to take the first few runs quite slowly and then as the chicken feels more relaxed, gradually to increase the pace. Soon the little feathered friends will be enjoying themselves enormously, laughing as only chickens can.

IMPORTANT REMINDER! *Get to know your chicken's parts* (see Fig 7)

After the trainee has reached its goal (represented as a target), it is time to wind the chicken back. GREAT CARE SHOULD BE TAKEN NOT TO FRIGHTEN THE BIRD. *Slow and steady* is the name of the game. Remember, being wound backwards can be disorienting. Having returned to the starting position it is time to start off again.

Exercise periods should be of no longer than 30 minutes duration.

Courses Available

The School of Aviary Aviation, later renamed the School of Fowl Training (SOFT) was located to the Northwest of Seattle. This independent body, wholly funded by private donations, not to be confused with the government sponsored Aerial Recruitment School of Endeavor (ARSE), offered scholarships and 100 positions to trainee flying chickens. The staff of twenty dedicated workers who operated the unique complex were intent on filling the skies with chickens as their motto so boldly stated: *Better to soar than be plucked.* Also located in the complex was the Aviary Store which sold all the accessories required for the flight program together with clan insignias such as Maltese Crosses and Buff Orpington comforters.

Do-it-yourself

For those who undertook self-training programs, the backyard became the place of learning. All over the city, enthusiasts constructed training machines and wound their feathered pupils to ever greater achievements.

Small groups would form to meet and compare notes and they soon became known as the "neighborcoop watchers". After two years of intense backyard manipulation these proud owners of flying fowls held their heads high. They stood and walked tall.

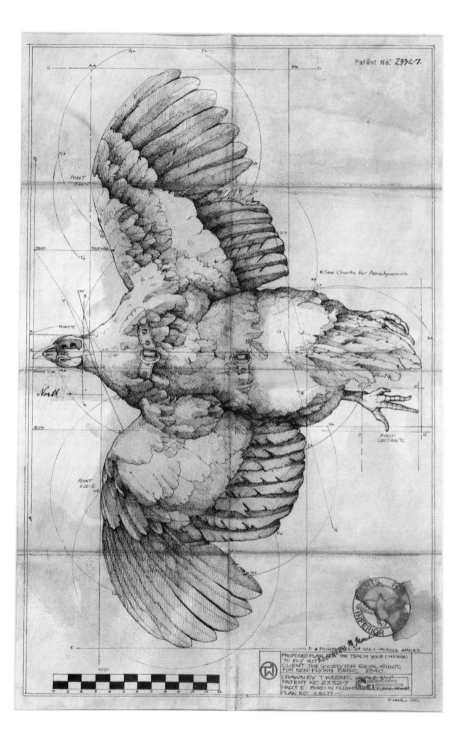

Figure 9.
This aerial view of the bird in flight graphically depicts the graceful wingspread of a chicken. However the fact that this particular fowl has lost one of its right secondary feathers may give it a slight propensity to veer off course.

25

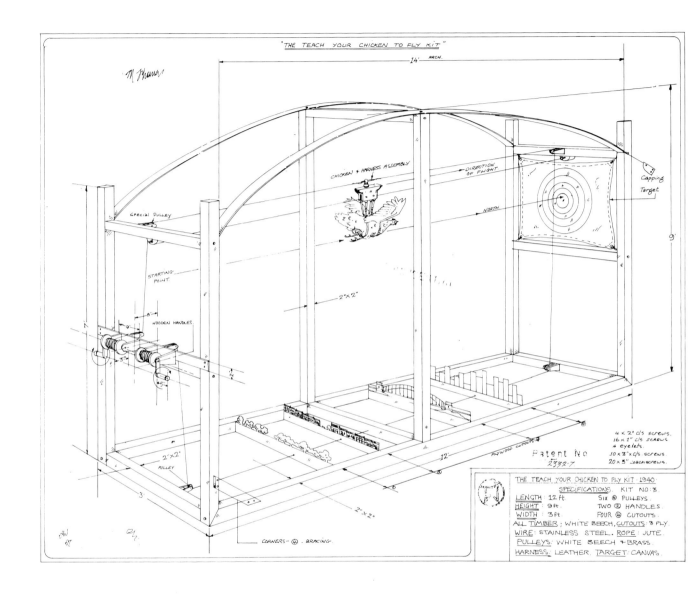

Figure 10.
A scale drawing of the "Teach Your Chicken To Fly" kit which was lodged with the patents office in 1940. A further 126 patents are either registered or pending for different designs relating to equipment used in fowl flight.

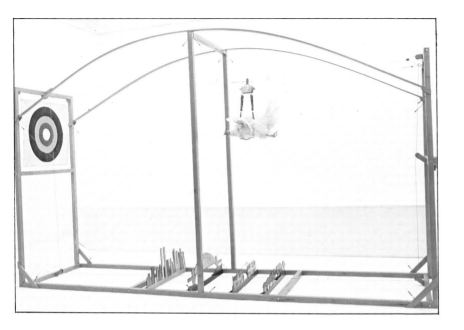

Figure 11a.
The flying machine in use.

Figure 11b.
The cutouts.

27

Figure 12.
An interesting flight angle taken in a wind tunnel by Mr. Trevor Weekes. The height of the wing flap is surprising considering the bodyweight/wingspan ratio of the average chicken.

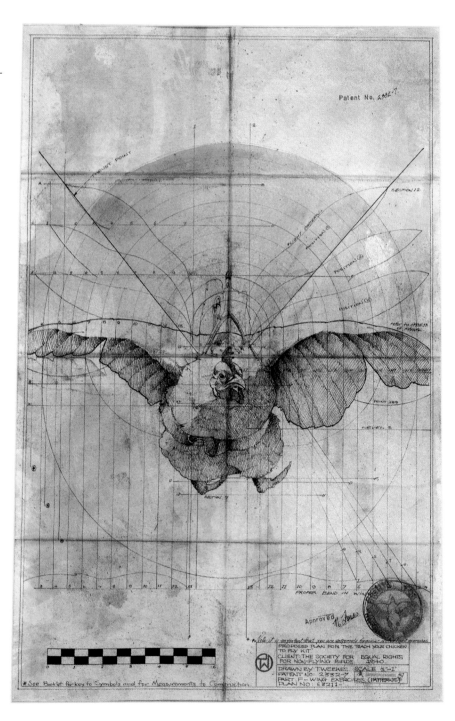

Figure 13.
The first aviator, Gregory Peck, seen
here having a morning work out
prior to his inaugural flight.

29

Figure 14.
An early photograph of Gregory Peck, the first chicken to fly. Photo kindly loaned by the Museum of Applied Sciences.

Accessories

5

Motorized Back Pack

A wind-up motor was designed to assist those chickens who wore goggles (see Fig.15). This piece of equipment was found necessary for high-flying chickens, many of whom suffered injury when foreign objects lodged in their eyes.

The main disadvantage of this motor was that the aviator needed to return to base after only five minutes flying time for a rewind.

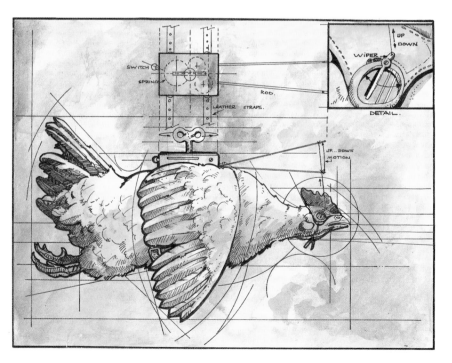

Figure 15.
Weight has always been of prime concern for users of the Motorized Back Pack. Originally made from titanium, recent developments in multi-cellular graphites have produced an ultra lightweight pack called the "Chickpack."

Starting Machine

This is an essential aid to the development of wing muscles in trainee flyers. By using the machine, chickens can gain valuable pre-flight experience in their own fowl yard without the risk of vertigo. It is solidly constructed, has a pilot mirror below the beak so that the chicken can reassure itself from its own image and can be worked by hand without an assistant. The Starting Machine comes free with Kit No. 4 (See Fig: 16 below).

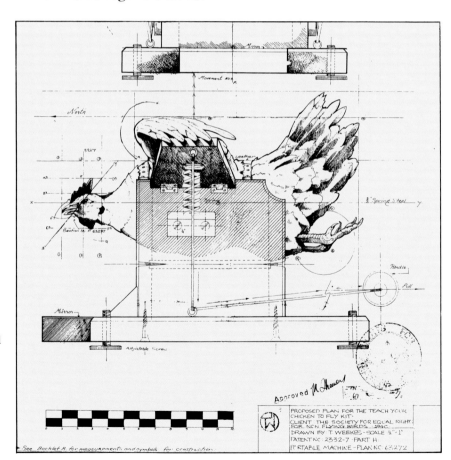

Figure 16.
The Starting Machine, which activates the bird's wings, should not be confused with the Flying Machine in which the fowl is encouraged to flap on its own. The Starting Machine is hand operated and is an optional extra. Care should be taken when operating the crank handle as excessive turning can cause repetitive strain injury usually referred to as "fowl flap syndrome."

Conclusions

6

The years between 1940 and 1953 were exciting ones and the School of Fowl Training went from strength to strength. Increasing numbers of poultry keepers and chicken fanciers felt that it was time for their feathered friends to leave the nest and aim for the sky. A total of 250 chickens graduated from the school, not to mention home-trained birds, and reports came in about sightings from all over the world. Free-range fowl flights were recorded from as far away as Japan, Brazil and even India.

The fowl flight training program took about six months to complete, allowing two months for each stage of the project. When it was felt by the instructors that their pupils were ready, they were taken to Big Sur, south of San Francisco, to see if they could actually sustain flight.

Big Sur provides substantial updraughts to aid chickens to take off... and take off they certainly did! The feeling of excitement at the first official testing could only have been matched by that epic day in 1903 when Orville Wright was lifted into the air above the rolling sand dunes at Kitty Hawk in North Carolina.

However despite the success of the training machine,

Figure 17.
Big Sur is a mecca for free flight, and has strong updrafts similar to those found at the cliffs of Dover in England.

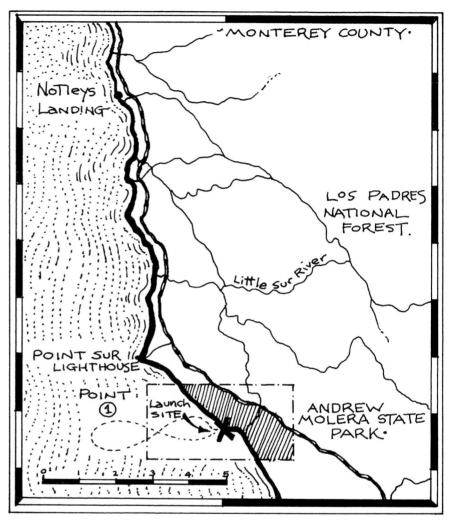

interest in fowl flying had flapped to a halt by 1953. Not until almost 30 years later, in April 1982, did they take to the air again. The event which sparked this rebirth was an exhibition of selected drawings together with the reconstruction of an original training kit. And so once again these splendid creatures grace our skies. Bird lovers of the world, unite! Let us all help the bird that evolution forgot.

Frontiers of Flight

After years of experimenting and intense work reconstructing the body, it was realized that the brain of the chicken also required improvement. A brain development program (Kit No. 62115) was established and X-rays were taken at the beginning of the program and again six months later. See Fig.18, below, which shows the comparison; proof positive that the program worked.

Figure 18.
X-rays of the chicken brain were provided courtesy of the Rhode Island Medical Center.

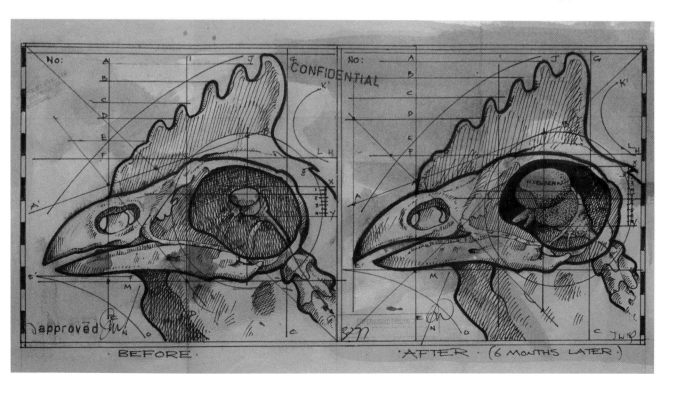

· BEFORE ·   ·AFTER · (6 MONTHS LATER.)